Favorite Piano Solos
for All Occasions

ISBN 978-1-4234-8211-6

HAL•LEONARD®
CORPORATION
7777 W. BLUEMOUND RD. P.O. BOX 13819 MILWAUKEE, WI 53213

For all works contained herein:
Unauthorized copying, arranging, adapting, recording, Internet posting, public performance,
or other distribution of the printed music in this publication is an infringement of copyright.
Infringers are liable under the law.

Visit Hal Leonard Online at
www.halleonard.com

CONTENTS

MOVIE/TELEVISON

NEW AGE

POP/ROCK

STANDARDS

MISCELLANEOUS

CAN'T HELP LOVIN' DAT MAN

from SHOW BOAT

Lyrics by OSCAR HAMMERSTEIN II
Music by JEROME KERN

Moderate Blues tempo ($\quad$ = 108)

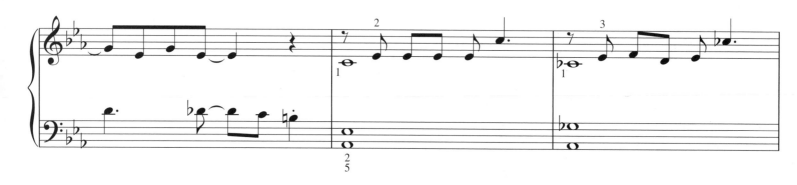

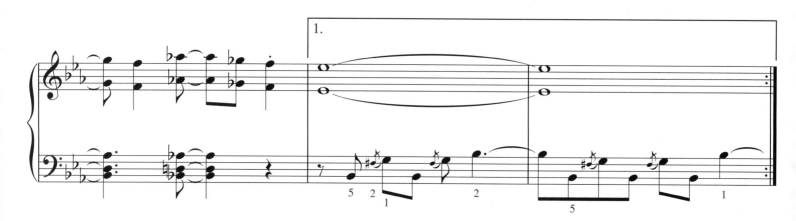

Copyright © 1927 UNIVERSAL - POLYGRAM INTERNATIONAL PUBLISHING, INC.
Copyright Renewed
This arrangement Copyright © 1992 UNIVERSAL - POLYGRAM INTERNATIONAL PUBLISHING, INC.
All Rights Reserved   Used by Permission

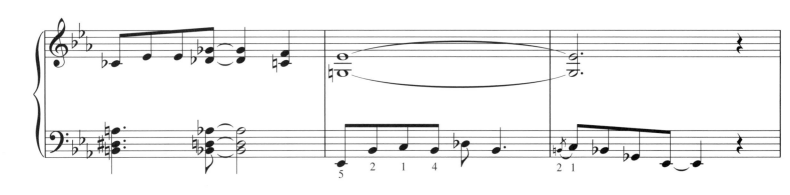

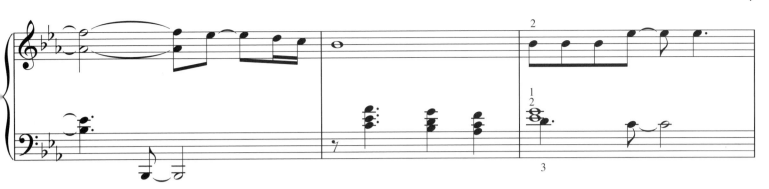

DEFYING GRAVITY

from the Broadway Musical WICKED

Music and Lyrics by
STEPHEN SCHWARTZ

Copyright © 2003 Greydog Music
This arrangement Copyright © 2008 Greydog Music
All Rights Reserved   Used by Permission

With determination

rall.

ff

DON'T CRY FOR ME ARGENTINA

from EVITA

Words by TIM RICE
Music by ANDREW LLOYD WEBBER

Freely

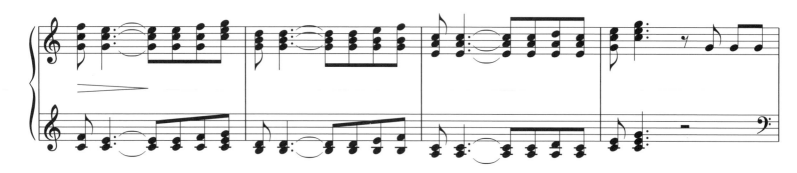

Moderately slow, rhythmic

Copyright © 1976, 1977 EVITA MUSIC LTD.
Copyright Renewed
This arrangement Copyright © 1998 EVITA MUSIC LTD.
All Rights for the United States and Canada Controlled and Administered by UNIVERSAL MUSIC CORP.
All Rights Reserved   Used by Permission

I'LL KNOW
from GUYS AND DOLLS

By FRANK LOESSER

© 1950 (Renewed) FRANK MUSIC CORP.
This arrangement © 2009 FRANK MUSIC CORP.
All Rights Reserved

LEARN TO BE LONELY
from THE PHANTOM OF THE OPERA

Music by ANDREW LLOYD WEBBER
Lyrics by CHARLES HART

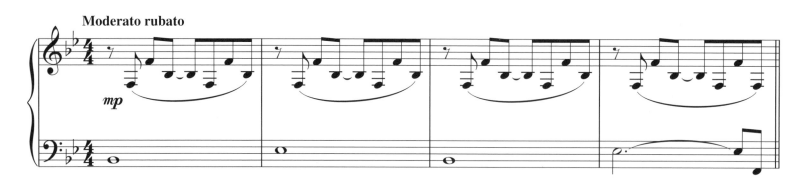

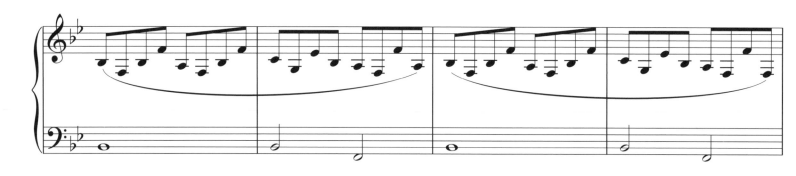

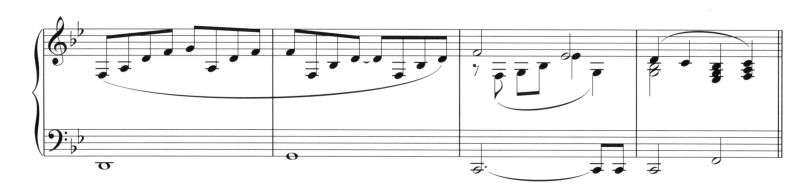

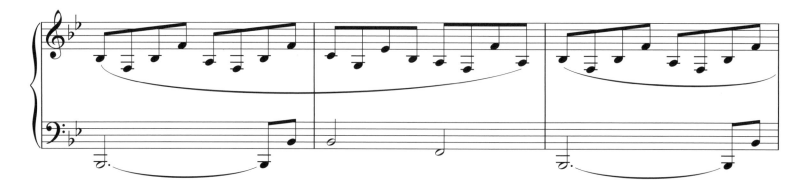

© Copyright 2004 Andrew Lloyd Webber licensed to The Really Useful Group Ltd.
This arrangement © Copyright 2005 Andrew Lloyd Webber licensed to The Really Useful Group Ltd.
International Copyright Secured   All Rights Reserved

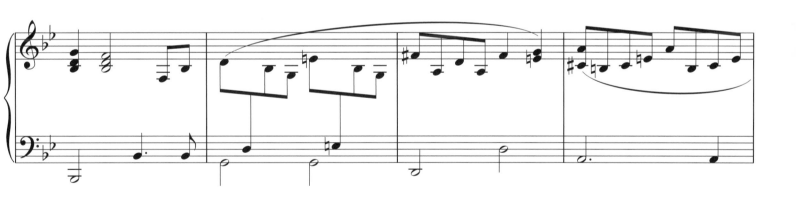

UNEXPECTED SONG

from SONG & DANCE

Music by ANDREW LLOYD WEBBER
Lyrics by DON BLACK

© Copyright 1978, 1982 Andrew Lloyd Webber licensed to The Really Useful Group Ltd.
This arrangement © Copyright 1993 Andrew Lloyd Webber licensed to The Really Useful Group Ltd.
International Copyright Secured   All Rights Reserved

SEASONS OF LOVE

from RENT

Words and Music by
JONATHAN LARSON

Moderate Ballad

Copyright © 1996 FINSTER & LUCY MUSIC LTD. CO.
This arrangement Copyright © 2003 FINSTER & LUCY MUSIC LTD. CO.
All Rights Controlled and Administered by UNIVERSAL MUSIC CORP.
All Rights Reserved   Used by Permission

34

A WONDERFUL GUY
from SOUTH PACIFIC

Lyrics by OSCAR HAMMERSTEIN II
Music by RICHARD RODGERS

Copyright © 1949 by Richard Rodgers and Oscar Hammerstein II
Copyright Renewed
This arrangement Copyright © 1988 by WILLIAMSON MUSIC
WILLIAMSON MUSIC owner of publication and allied rights throughout the world
International Copyright Secured All Rights Reserved

Tempo I°

HALLELUJAH CHORUS
from MESSIAH

By GEORGE FRIDERIC HANDEL

Allegro moderato

Copyright © 1999 by HAL LEONARD CORPORATION
International Copyright Secured   All Rights Reserved

43

45

AIR
Theme from the "Goldberg" Variations

By JOHANN SEBASTIAN BACH

Andante espressivo

Copyright © 2001 by HAL LEONARD CORPORATION
International Copyright Secured   All Rights Reserved

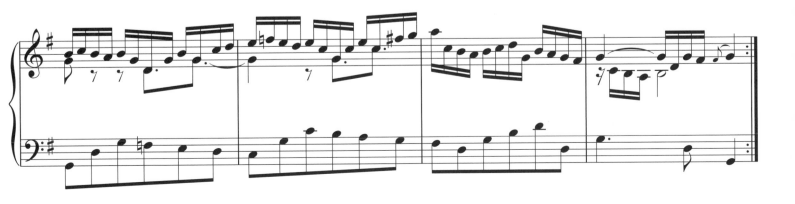

GREENSLEEVES

Sixteenth Century Traditional English

Gently

Copyright © 2010 by HAL LEONARD CORPORATION
International Copyright Secured   All Rights Reserved

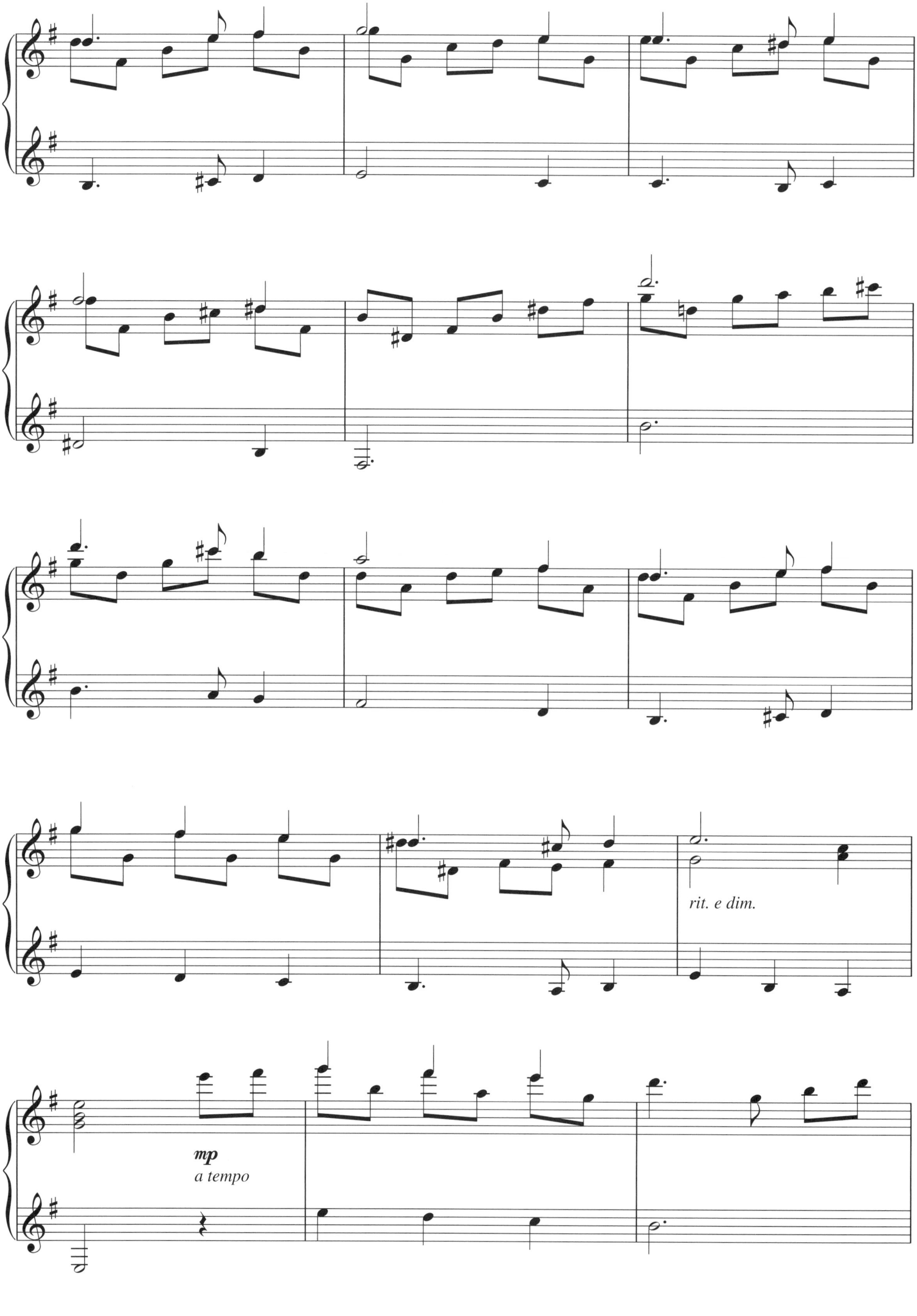
rit. e dim.
mp
a tempo

ODE TO JOY
from SYMPHONY NO. 9 IN D MINOR

By LUDWIG VAN BEETHOVEN

With spirit

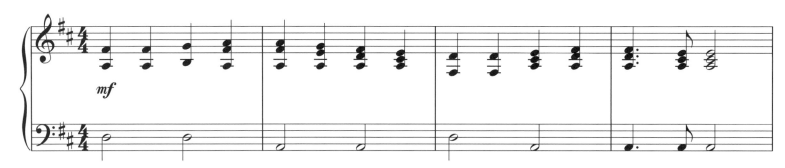

Copyright © 2004 by HAL LEONARD CORPORATION
International Copyright Secured   All Rights Reserved

SYMPHONY NO. 9
("From The New World"), Second Movement Excerpt

By ANTONÍN DVOŘÁK

Copyright © 1998 by HAL LEONARD CORPORATION
International Copyright Secured   All Rights Reserved

BILLIE'S BOUNCE
(Bill's Bounce)

By CHARLIE PARKER

Copyright © 1945 (Renewed 1973) Atlantic Music Corp.
This arrangement Copyright © 2001 Atlantic Music Corp.
All Rights for the World excluding the U.S. Controlled and Administered by Screen Gems-EMI Music Inc.
International Copyright Secured   All Rights Reserved

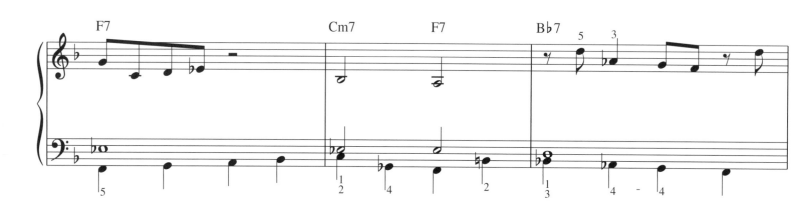

ALL OF ME

Words and Music by SEYMOUR SIMONS
and GERALD MARKS

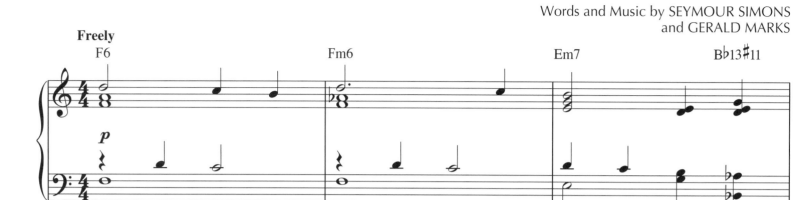

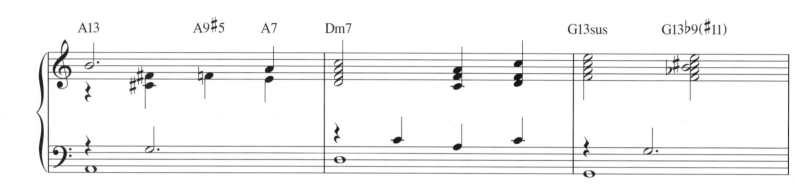

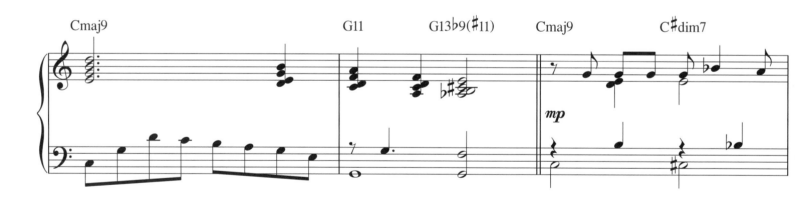

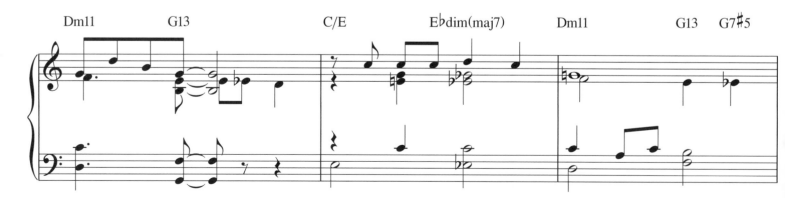

Copyright © 1931 Sony/ATV Music Publishing LLC, Gerald Marks Music and Marlong Music Corp.
Copyright Renewed
This arrangement Copyright © 2009 Sony/ATV Music Publishing LLC, Gerald Marks Music and Marlong Music Corp.
All Rights on behalf of Sony/ATV Music Publishing LLC and Gerald Marks Music Administered by Sony/ATV Music Publishing LLC, 8 Music Square West, Nashville, TN 37203
International Copyright Secured   All Rights Reserved

63

NUAGES

By DJANGO REINHARDT
and JACQUES LARUE

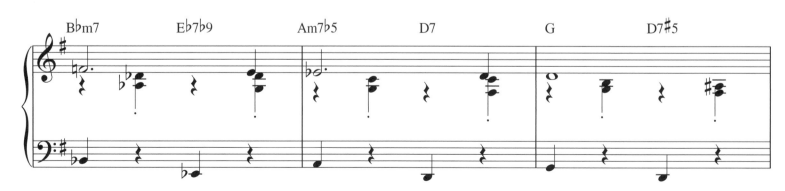

© 1980 PETER MAURICE MUSIC LTD.
This arrangement Copyright © 2010 PETER MAURICE MUSIC LTD.
All Rights for the U.S. and Canada Controlled and Administered by COLGEMS-EMI MUSIC INC.
All Rights Reserved   International Copyright Secured   Used by Permission

68

Adapted from a Django Reinhardt solo

POOR BUTTERFLY

Words by JOHN L. GOLDEN
Music by RAYMOND HUBBELL

Slowly, with expression

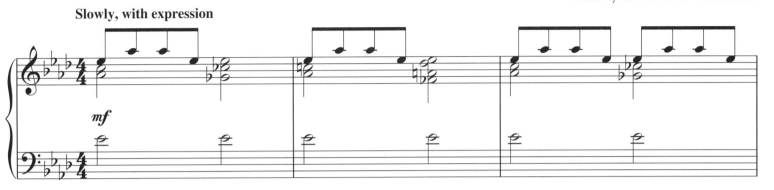

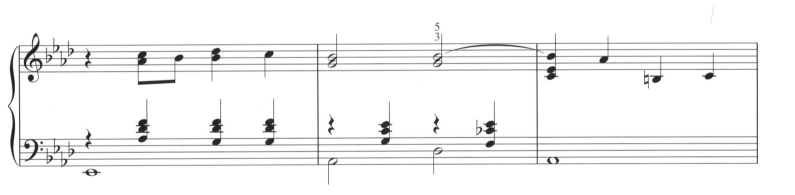

Copyright © 2010 by HAL LEONARD CORPORATION
International Copyright Secured   All Rights Reserved

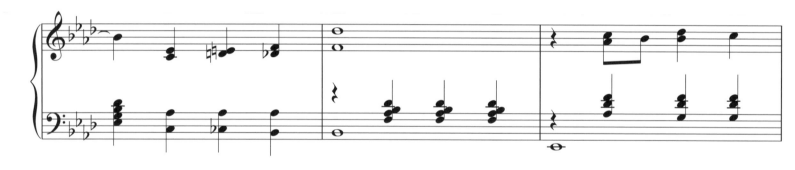

SUNNY

Words and Music by
BOBBY HEBB

Copyright © 1966 Portable Music Company, Inc.
Copyright Renewed
This arrangement Copyright © 2008 Portable Music Company, Inc.
All Rights Administered by Chrysalis Songs
All Rights Reserved   Used by Permission

WALTZ FOR DEBBY

Lyric by GENE LEES
Music by BILL EVANS

TRO - © Copyright 1964 (Renewed), 1965 (Renewed), 1966 (Renewed) Folkways Music Publishers, Inc., New York, NY
This arrangement TRO - © Copyright 2001 Folkways Music Publishers, Inc.
International Copyright Secured
All Rights Reserved Including Public Performance For Profit
Used by Permission

AQUELLOS OJOS VERDES
(Green Eyes)

Music by NILO MENENDEZ
Spanish Words by ADOLFO UTRERA
English Words by E. RIVERA and E. WOODS

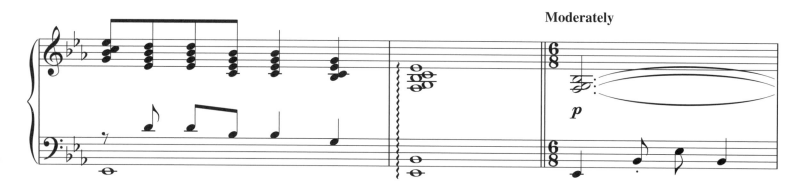

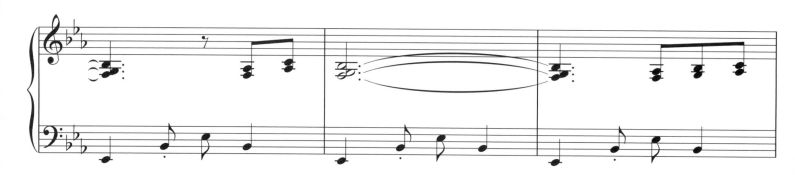

Copyright © 1929, 1931 by Peer International Corporation
Copyrights Renewed
This arrangement Copyright © 2004 by Peer International Corporation
International Copyright Secured   All Rights Reserved

A Tempo Bossa Nova

CAST YOUR FATE TO THE WIND

Music by
VINCE GUARALDI

Copyright © 1961 by David Guaraldi Music and Dia Guaraldi Music
Copyright Renewed
This arrangement Copyright © 2001 by David Guaraldi Music and Dia Guaraldi Music
All Rights Administered by Hogan Media & Music, Inc.
All Rights Reserved   Used by Permission

Open Repeat

A♭   D♭   E♭   D♭

(solo ad lib.)

With heavy pedal to end

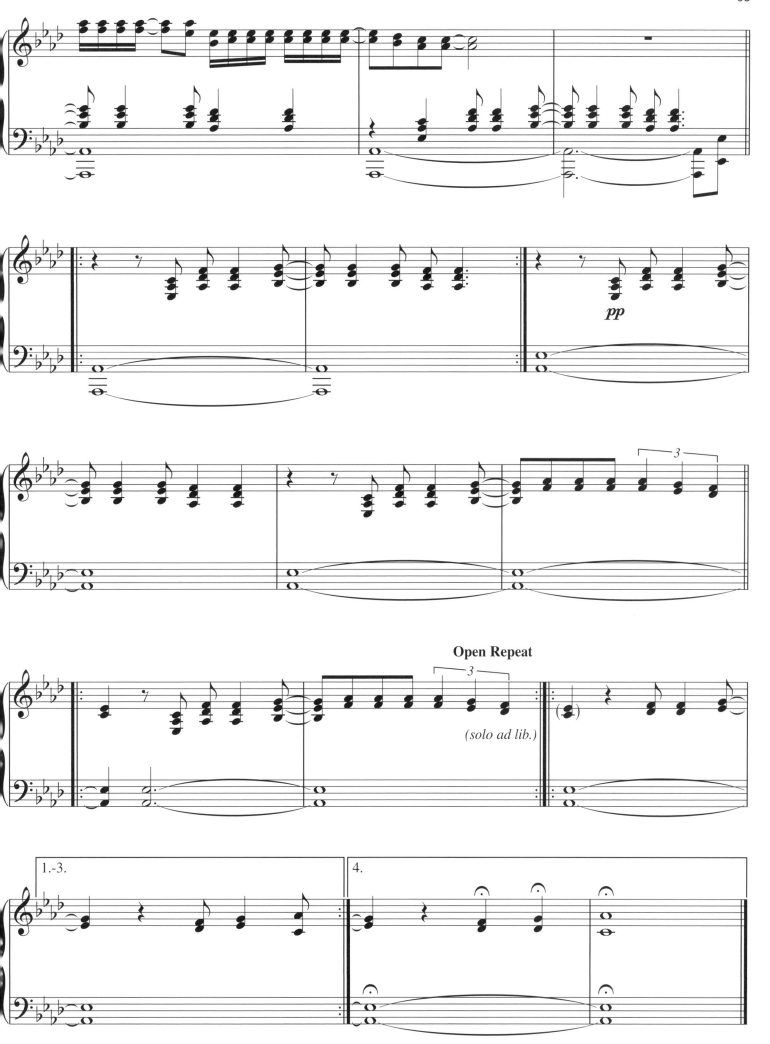

Open Repeat

(solo ad lib.)

1.-3.

4.

EL CHOCLO

Spanish Lyrics by FRANCIA LUBAN
English Lyrics by MARJORIE HARPER
Music by A.G. VILLOLDO

With intensity

Copyright © 1933 by Edward B. Marks Music Company
Copyright Renewed
This arrangement Copyright © 1998 by Edward B. Marks Music Company
International Copyright Secured   All Rights Reserved
Used by Permission

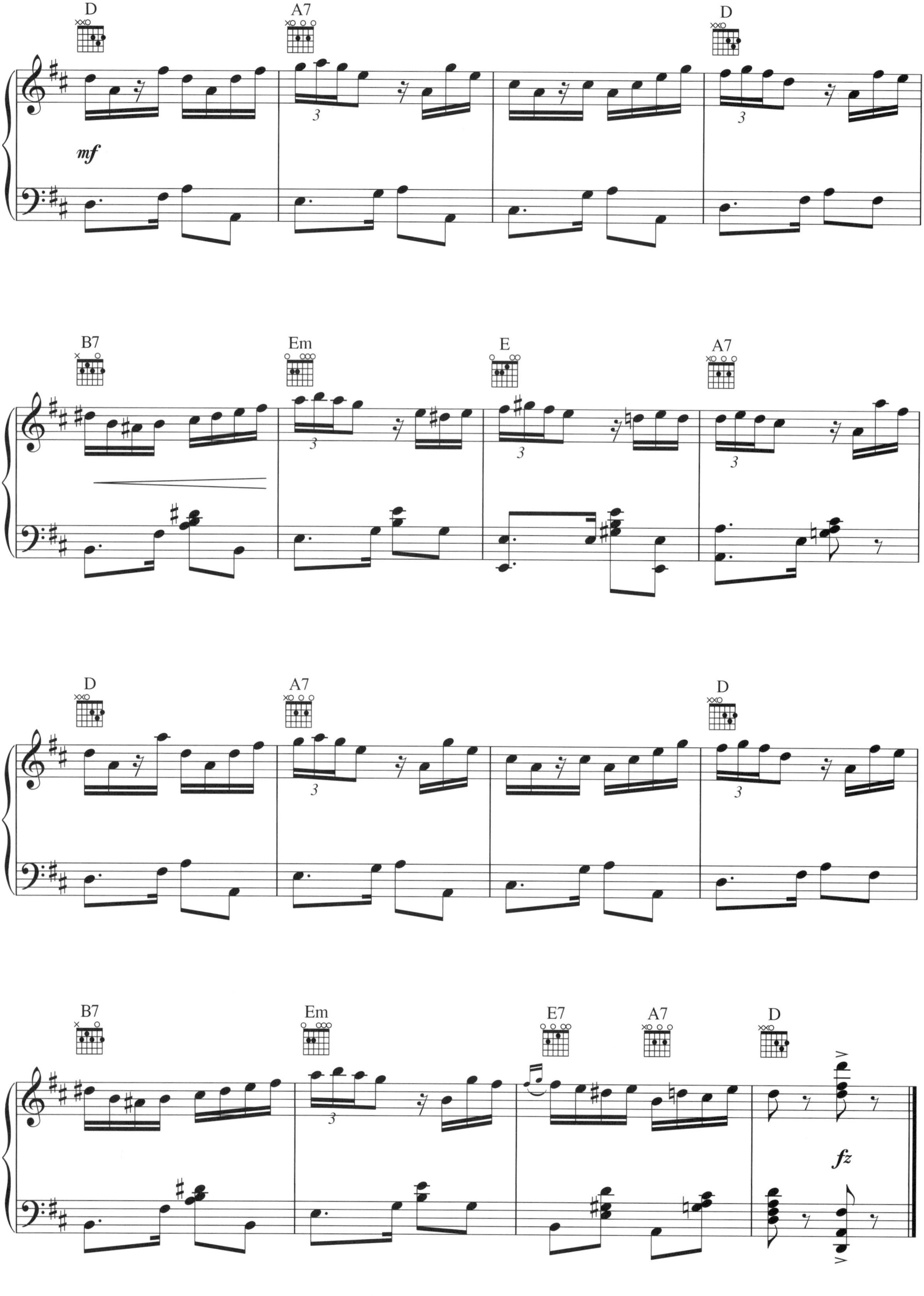
D
A7
D
mf
B7
Em
E
A7
D
A7
D
B7
Em
E7
A7
D
fz

IT'S IMPOSSIBLE
(Somos Novios)

English Lyric by SID WAYNE
Spanish Words and Music by
ARMANDO MANZANERO

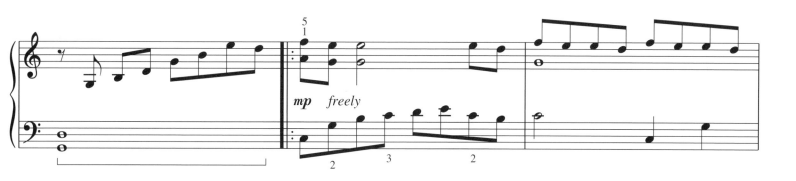

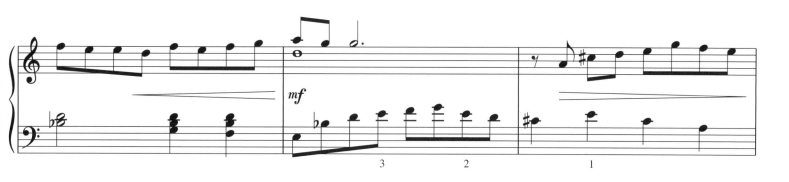

Copyright © 1968 by Universal Music Publishing MGB Edim., S.A. de C.V.
Copyright Renewed
This arrangement Copyright © 1995 by Universal Music Publishing MGB Edim., S.A. de C.V.
All Rights for the U.S.A. Administered by Universal Music - MGB Songs
International Copyright Secured   All Rights Reserved

MAMBO #5

Words and Music by
DAMASO PÉREZ PRADO

Bright Mambo

Copyright © 1948 by Editorial Mexicana de Musica Internacional, S.A.
Copyright Renewed
This arrangement Copyright © 2001 by Editorial Mexicana de Musica Internacional, S.A.
All Rights Administered by Peer International Corporation
International Copyright Secured   All Rights Reserved

WAVE

Words and Music by
ANTONIO CARLOS JOBIM

Copyright © 1967, 1968 Antonio Carlos Jobim
Copyright Renewed
This arrangement Copyright © 2004 Antonio Carlos Jobim
Published by Corcovado Music Corp.
International Copyright Secured   All Rights Reserved

With pedal

I WILL ALWAYS LOVE YOU

Words and Music by
DOLLY PARTION

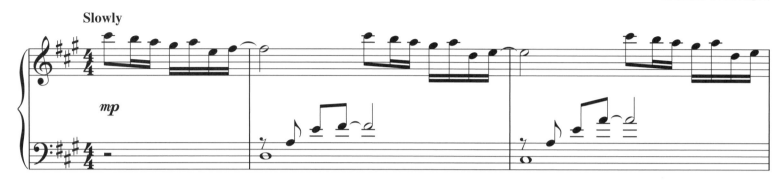

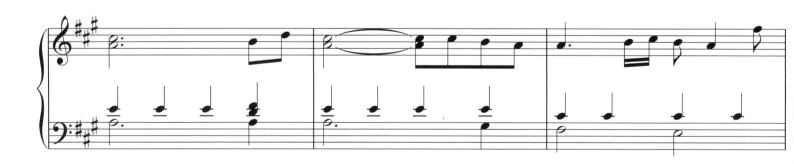

Copyright © 1973 (Renewed 2001) Velvet Apple Music
This arrangement Copyright © 2009 Velvet Apple Music
All Rights Reserved   Used by Permission

IF

Words and Music by
DAVID GATES

Moderately and lyrically

Copyright © 1971 Sony/ATV Music Publishing LLC
Copyright Renewed
This arrangement Copyright © 1994 Sony/ATV Music Publishing LLC
All Rights Administered by Sony/ATV Music Publishing LLC, 8 Music Square West, Nashville, TN 37203
International Copyright Secured   All Rights Reserved

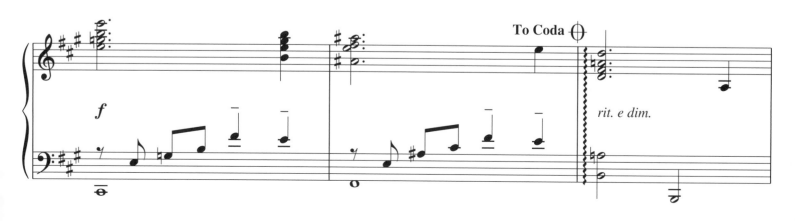

IF YOU GO AWAY

French Words and Music by JACQUES BREL
English Words by ROD McKUEN

Moderate French Waltz
(poco rubato throughout)

Copyright © 1959, 1966 by Edward B. Marks Music Company
Copyright Renewed
This arrangement Copyright © 1984 by Edward B. Marks Music Company
International Copyright Secured   All Rights Reserved
Used by Permission

119

122

YOU ARE THE SUNSHINE OF MY LIFE

Words and Music by
STEVIE WONDER

Moderately, with feeling

© 1972 (Renewed 2000) JOBETE MUSIC CO., INC. and BLACK BULL MUSIC
c/o EMI APRIL MUSIC INC.
This arrangement © 2009 JOBETE MUSIC CO., INC. and BLACK BULL MUSIC
c/o EMI APRIL MUSIC INC.
All Rights Reserved   International Copyright Secured   Used by Permission

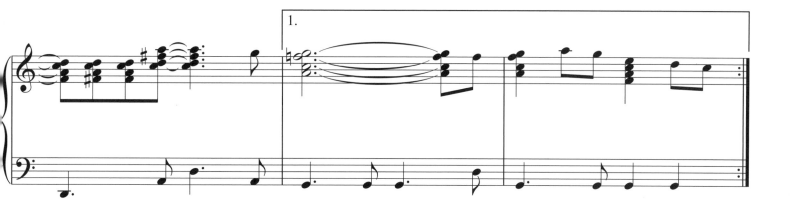

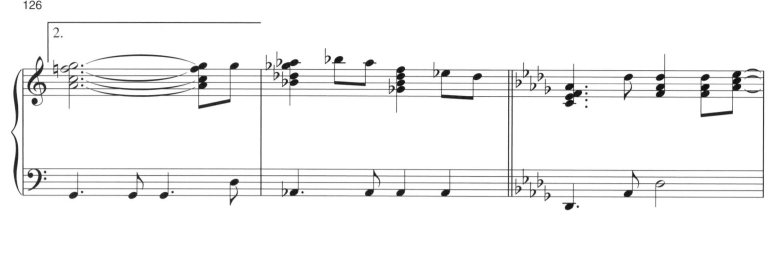

rit.

a tempo

1.

2.

rit.

ANGELA
Theme from the Paramount Television Series TAXI

By BOB JAMES

Copyright © 1979 Addax Music Company Inc. and Remidi Music
This arrangement Copyright © 2005 Addax Music Company Inc. and Remidi Music
All Rights Administered by Sony/ATV Music Publishing LLC, 8 Music Square West, Nashville, TN 37203
International Copyright Secured   All Rights Reserved

Without pedal

ATONEMENT
from ATONEMENT

By DARIO MARIANELLI

Con Rubato ♩ = c. 50

Copyright © 2007 UNIVERSAL PICTURES MUSIC
This arrangement Copyright © 2007 UNIVERSAL PICTURES MUSIC
All Rights Controlled and Administered by UNIVERSAL MUSIC CORP.
All Rights Reserved   Used by Permission

BELLA'S LULLABY
from the Summit Entertainment film TWILIGHT

Composed by CARTER BURWELL

Moderately

Copyright © 2008 by Summit Entertainment LLC
This arrangement Copyright © 2009 by Summit Entertainment LLC
All Rights Reserved   Used by Permission

BRIAN'S SONG
Theme from the Screen Gems Television Production BRIAN'S SONG

Music by
MICHEL LEGRAND

© 1972 (Renewed 2000) COLGEMS-EMI MUSIC INC.
This Arrangement © 1994 COLGEMS-EMI MUSIC INC.
All Rights Reserved   International Copyright Secured   Used by Permission

CINEMA PARADISO

from CINEMA PARADISO

Music by ENNIO MORRICONE

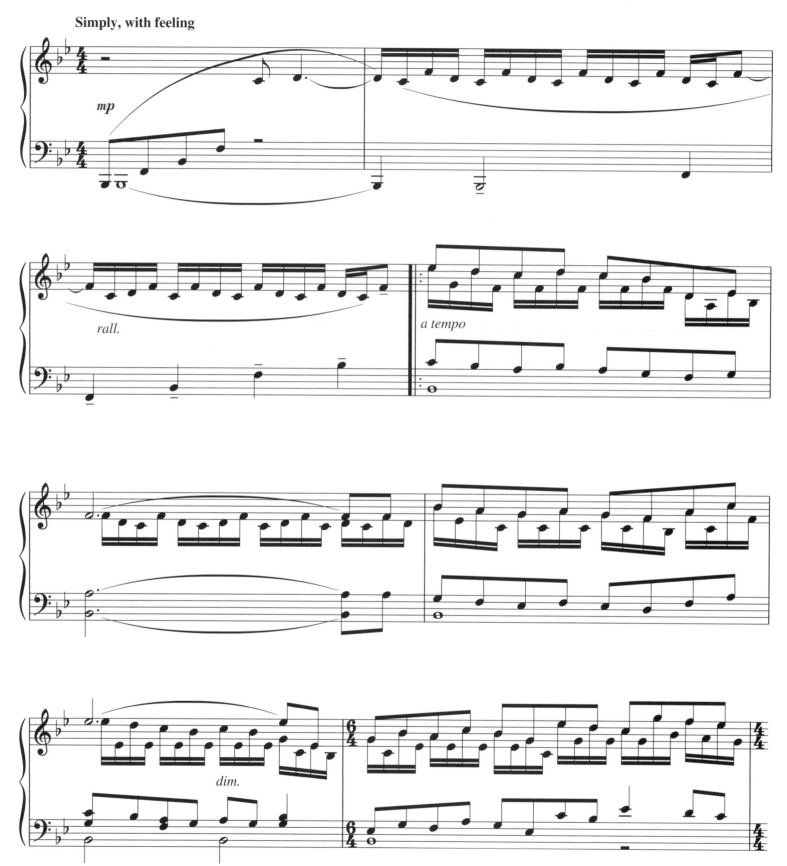

© 1988 EMI GENERAL MUSIC SRL
This arrangement © 1996 EMI GENERAL MUSIC SRL
All Rights Controlled and Administered by EMI APRIL MUSIC INC.
All Rights Reserved   International Copyright Secured   Used by Permission

COLORS OF THE WIND

from Walt Disney's POCAHONTAS

Music by ALAN MENKEN
Lyrics by STEPHEN SCHWARTZ

© 1995 Wonderland Music Company, Inc. and Walt Disney Music Company
This arrangement © 1995 Wonderland Music Company, Inc. and Walt Disney Music Company
All Rights Reserved   Used by Permission

THE EXODUS THEME

from EXODUS

Words and Music by
ERNEST GOLD

Slowly and expressively

Copyright © 1960 by Carlyle-Alpina Edition
Copyright Renewed
This arrangement Copyright © 1981 by Carlyle-Alpina Edition
All Rights Administered by Chappell & Co.
International Copyright Secured   All Rights Reserved

HE'S A PIRATE

from Walt Disney Pictures' PIRATES OF THE CARIBBEAN: THE CURSE OF THE BLACK PEARL

Music by KLAUS BADELT

Briskly

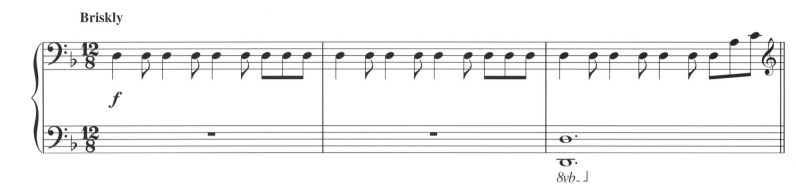

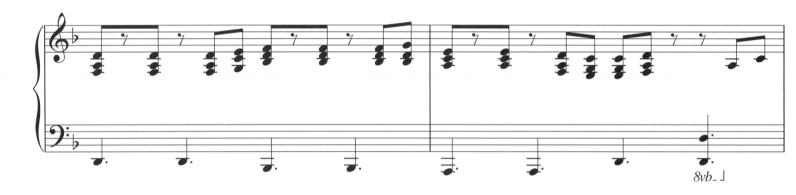

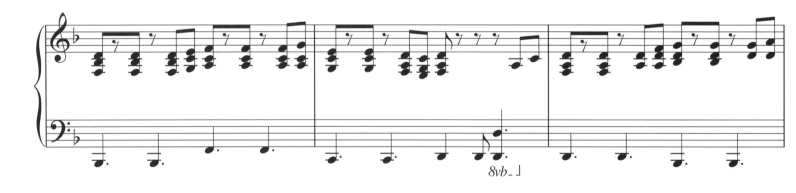

© 2003 Walt Disney Music Company
This arrangement © 2003 Walt Disney Music Company
All Rights Reserved   Used by Permission

THE KRAKEN

from Walt Disney Pictures' PIRATES OF THE CARIBBEAN: DEAD MAN'S CHEST

Music by HANS ZIMMER

Slow and steady

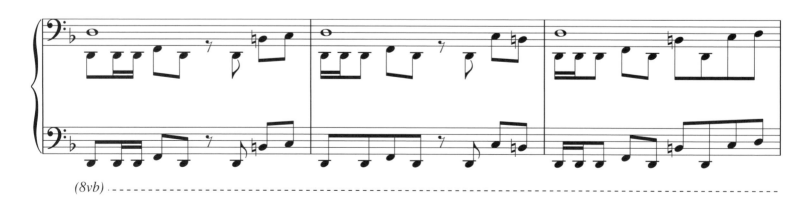

© 2006 Walt Disney Music Company
This arrangement © 2006 Walt Disney Music Company
All Rights Reserved   Used by Permission

159

8vb -

No pedal

(8vb) -

(8vb) -

LINUS AND LUCY

By VINCE GUARALDI

Moderately

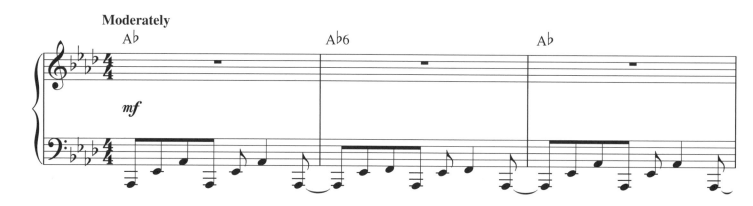

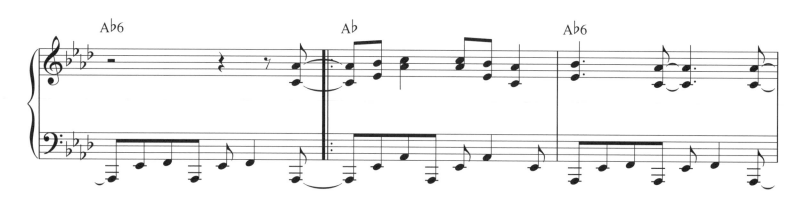

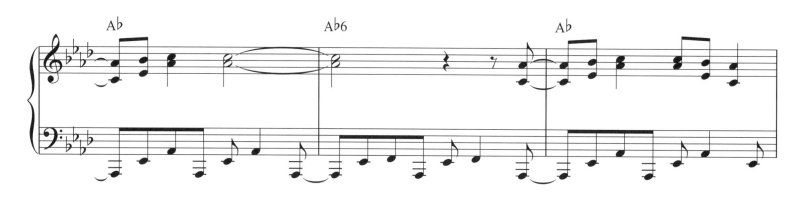

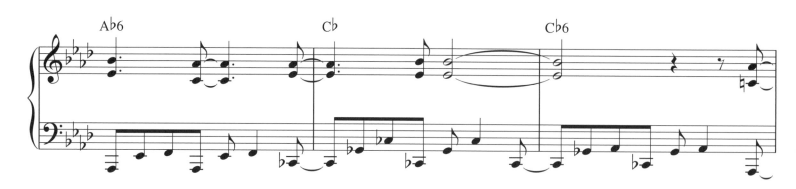

Copyright © 1965 LEE MENDELSON FILM PRODUCTIONS, INC.
Copyright Renewed
This arrangement Copyright © 2004 LEE MENDELSON FILM PRODUCTIONS, INC.
International Copyright Secured   All Rights Reserved

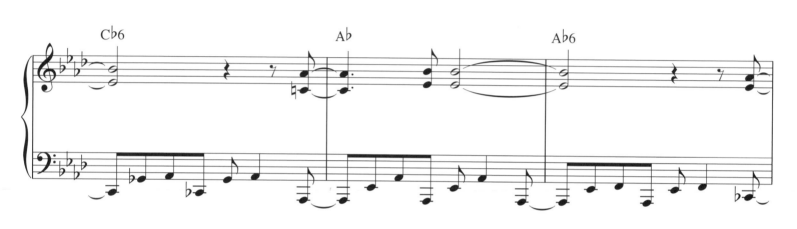

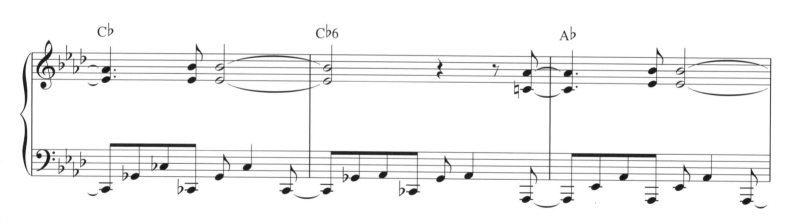

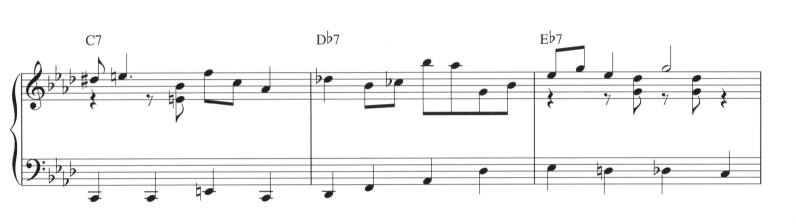

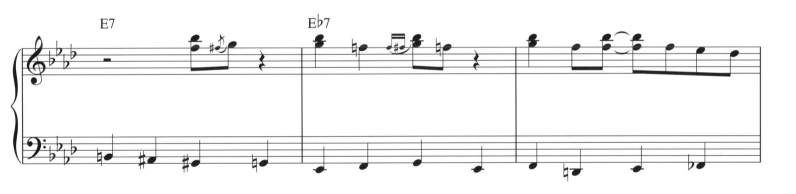

WE'RE ALL IN THIS TOGETHER

from the Disney Channel Original Movie HIGH SCHOOL MUSICAL

Words and Music by MATTHEW GERRARD
and ROBBIE NEVIL

© 2005 Walt Disney Music Company
This arrangement © 2008 Walt Disney Music Company
All Rights Reserved   Used by Permission

CODA

NEW MOON
(The Meadow)
from the Summit Entertainment Film THE TWILIGHT SAGA: NEW MOON

Composed by
ALEXANDRE DESPLAT

Copyright © 2009 by Summit Base Camp Film Music
This arrangement Copyright © 2009 by Summit Base Camp Film Music
All Rights Reserved   Used by Permission

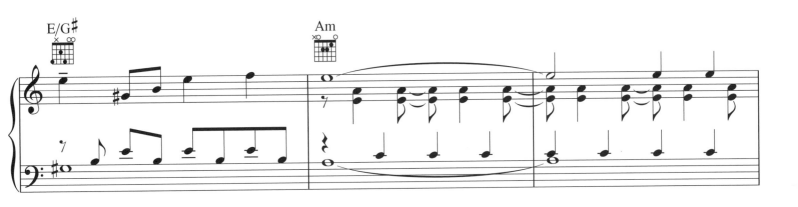

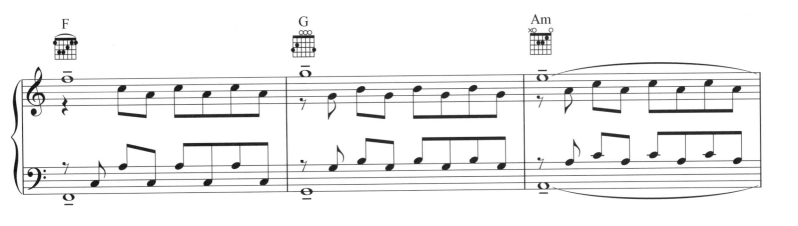

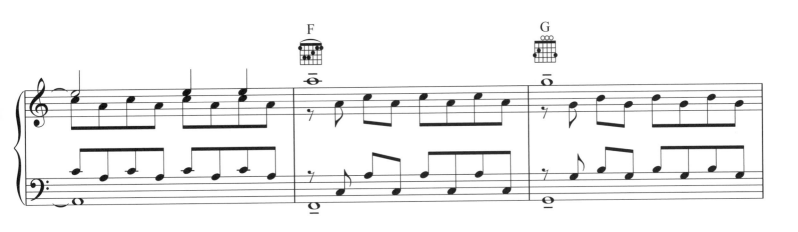

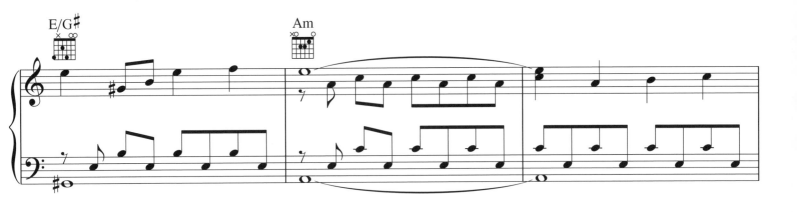

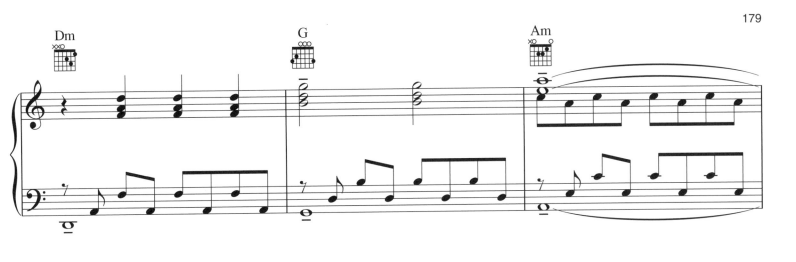

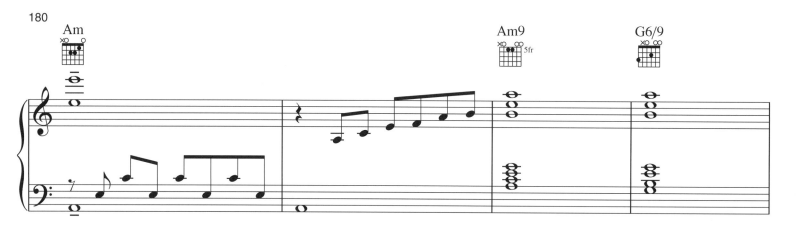

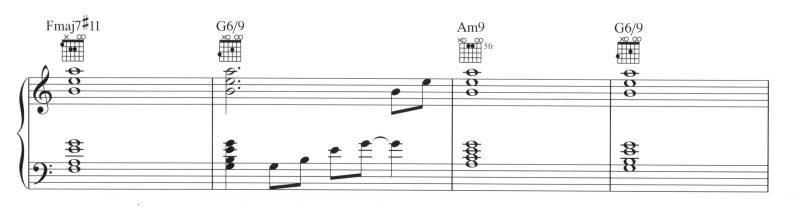

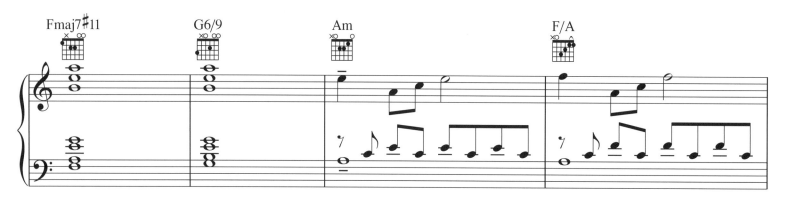

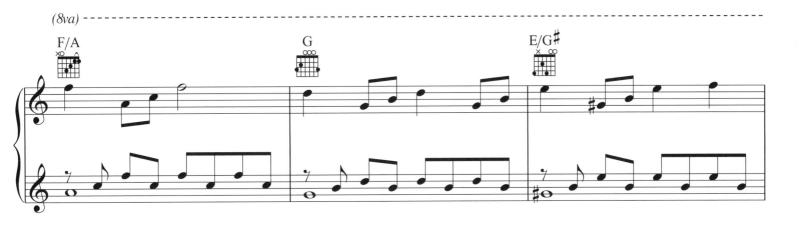

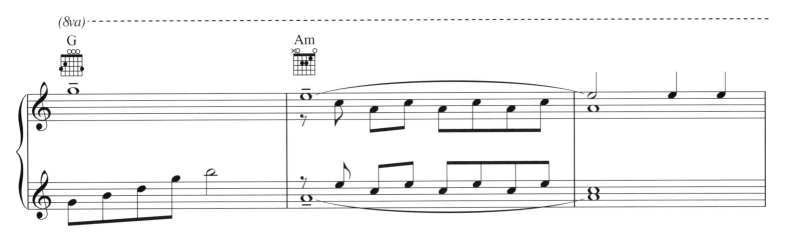

CHARIOTS OF FIRE

from CHARIOTS OF FIRE

Music by VANGELIS

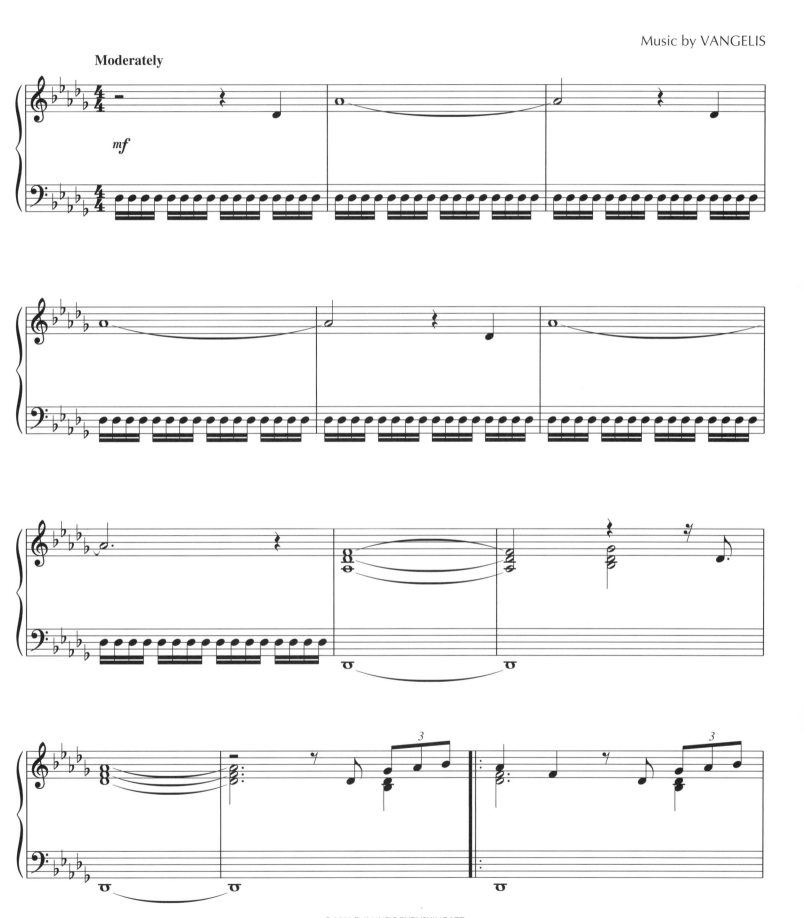

© 1981 EMI MUSIC PUBLISHING LTD.
This arrangement © 1994 EMI MUSIC PUBLISHING LTD.
All Rights for the World, excluding Holland, Controlled and Administered by EMI APRIL MUSIC INC.
All Rights Reserved   International Copyright Secured   Used by Permission

HYMNE

By VANGELIS

© 1977 (Renewed 2005) EMI MUSIC PUBLISHING LTD.
This arrangement © 1994 EMI MUSIC PUBLISHING LTD.
All Rights Controlled and Administered by EMI APRIL MUSIC INC.
All Rights Reserved   International Copyright Secured   Used by Permission

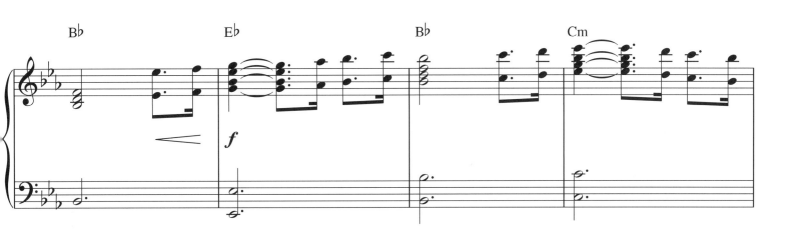

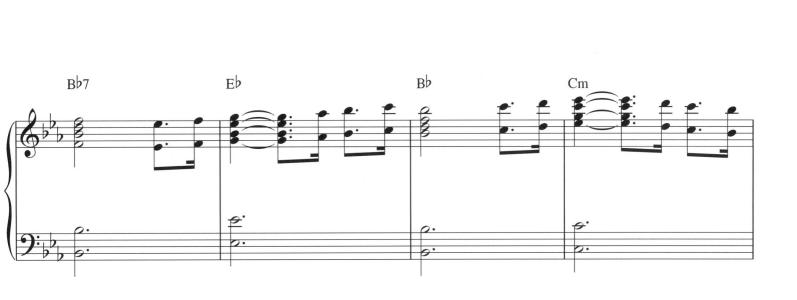

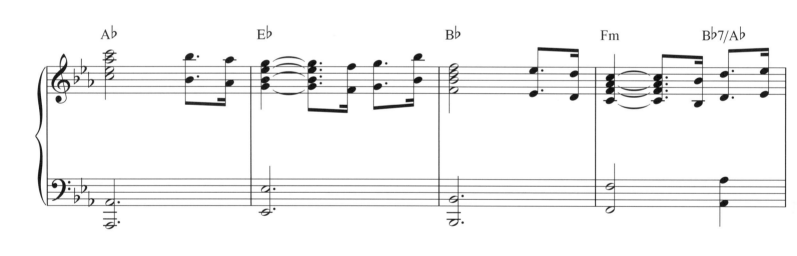

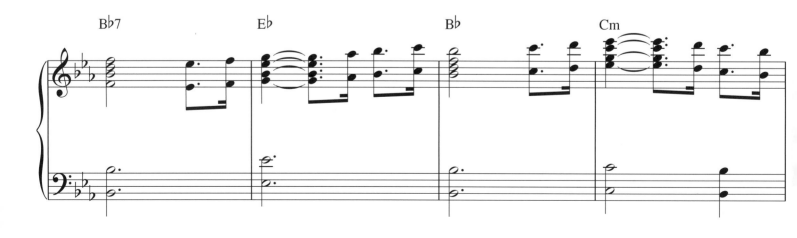

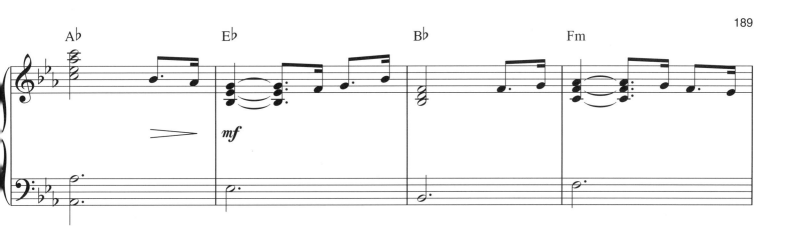

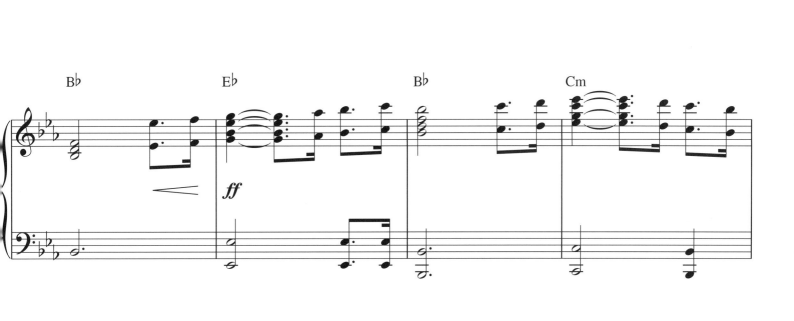

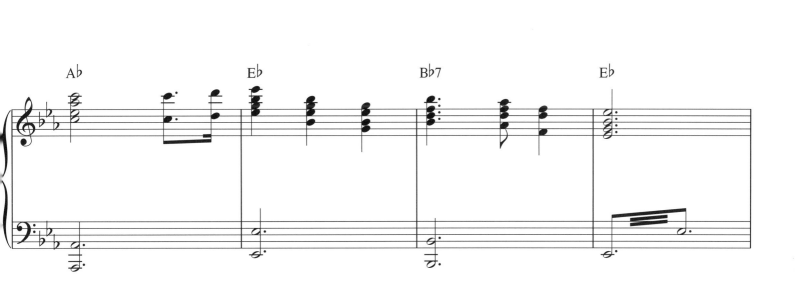

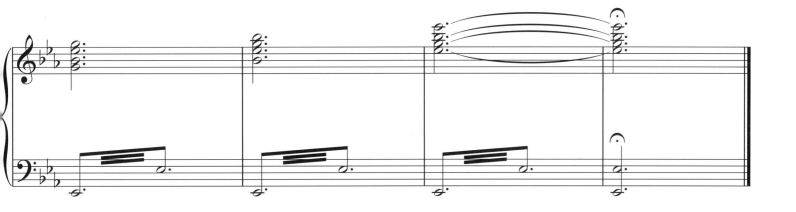

WATERMARK

Music by ENYA
Words by ROMA RYAN

Slowly, with rubato

With pedal

© 1989 EMI MUSIC PUBLISHING LTD.
This arrangement © 2010 EMI MUSIC PUBLISHING LTD.
All Rights Controlled and Administered by EMI BLACKWOOD MUSIC INC.
All Rights Reserved   International Copyright Secured   Used by Permission

ALL YOU NEED IS LOVE

Words and Music by JOHN LENNON
and PAUL McCARTNEY

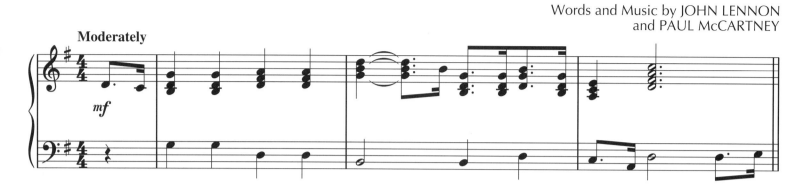

Copyright © 1967 Sony/ATV Music Publishing LLC
Copyright Renewed
This arrangement © 1995 Sony/ATV Music Publishing LLC
All Rights Administered by Sony/ATV Music Publishing LLC, 8 Music Square West, Nashville, TN 37203
International Copyright Secured   All Rights Reserved

To Coda $\oplus$

195

AND SO IT GOES

Words and Music by
BILLY JOEL

Rubato

© 1983 JOEL SONGS
This arrangement © 2001 JOEL SONGS
All Rights Reserved   International Copyright Secured   Used by Permission

BLACKBIRD

Words and Music by JOHN LENNON
and PAUL McCARTNEY

Slowly and smoothly

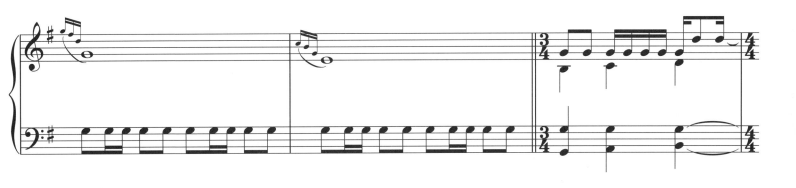

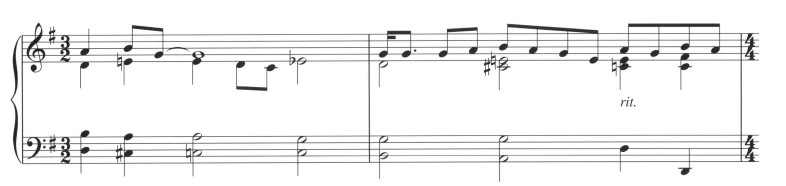

Copyright © 1968, 1969 Sony/ATV Music Publishing LLC
Copyright Renewed
This arrangement Copyright © 2009 Sony/ATV Music Publishing LLC
All Rights Administered by Sony/ATV Music Publishing LLC, 8 Music Square West, Nashville, TN 37203
International Copyright Secured   All Rights Reserved

BREATHE

Words and Music by HOLLY LAMAR
and STEPHANIE BENTLEY

Moderate Ballad, in 2

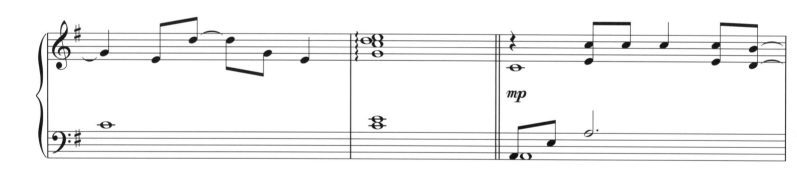

Copyright © 1999 Cal IV Songs, Universal - Songs Of PolyGram International, Inc. and Hopechest Music
This arrangement Copyright © 2006 Cal IV Songs, Universal - Songs Of PolyGram International, Inc. and Hopechest Music
All Rights on behalf of Cal IV Songs Administered by Cal IV Entertainment, Inc., 808 19th Avenue South, Nashville, TN 37203
All Rights on behalf of Hopechest Music Controlled and Administered by Universal - Songs Of PolyGram International, Inc.
All Rights Reserved   Used by Permission

210

WE ARE THE CHAMPIONS

Words and Music by
FREDDIE MERCURY

Moderately slow

© 1977 (Renewed 2005) QUEEN MUSIC LTD.
This arrangement © 1994 QUEEN MUSIC LTD.
All Rights for the U.S. and Canada Controlled and Administered by BEECHWOOD MUSIC CORP.
All Rights for the world excluding the U.S. and Canada Controlled and Administered by EMI MUSIC PUBLISHING LTD.
All Rights Reserved   International Copyright Secured   Used by Permission

213

CAN'T SMILE WITHOUT YOU

Words and Music by CHRIS ARNOLD,
DAVID MARTIN and GEOFF MORROW

Moderately, with a relaxed beat

Copyright © 1975 UNIVERSAL/DICK JAMES MUSIC LTD.
Copyright Renewed
This arrangement Copyright © 1999 UNIVERSAL/DICK JAMES MUSIC LTD.
All Rights in the U.S. and Canada Controlled and Administered by UNIVERSAL - SONGS OF POLYGRAM INTERNATIONAL, INC.
All Rights Reserved   Used by Permission

CANDLE IN THE WIND

Words and Music by ELTON JOHN
and BERNIE TAUPIN

Copyright © 1973 UNIVERSAL/DICK JAMES MUSIC LTD.
Copyright Renewed
This arrangement Copyright © 2009 UNIVERSAL/DICK JAMES MUSIC LTD.
All Rights in the United States and Canada Controlled and Administered by UNIVERSAL - SONGS OF POLYGRAM INTERNATIONAL, INC.
All Rights Reserved   Used by Permission

I WILL REMEMBER YOU

Theme from THE BROTHERS McMULLEN

Words and Music by SARAH McLACHLAN,
SEAMUS EGAN and DAVE MERENDA

Moderately slow

Copyright © 1995 Sony/ATV Music Publishing LLC, Tyde Music, Seamus Egan Music and T C F Music Publishing, Inc.
This arrangement Copyright © 2005 Sony/ATV Music Publishing LLC, Tyde Music, Seamus Egan Music and T C F Music Publishing, Inc.
All Rights on behalf of Sony/ATV Music Publishing LLC and Tyde Music Administered by Sony/ATV Music Publishing LLC, 8 Music Square West, Nashville, TN 37203
All Rights on behalf of Seamus Egan Music Administered by Fox Film Music Corp.
International Copyright Secured   All Rights Reserved

227

PIANO MAN

Words and Music by
BILLY JOEL

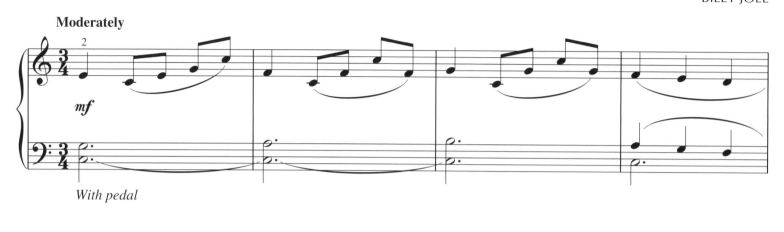

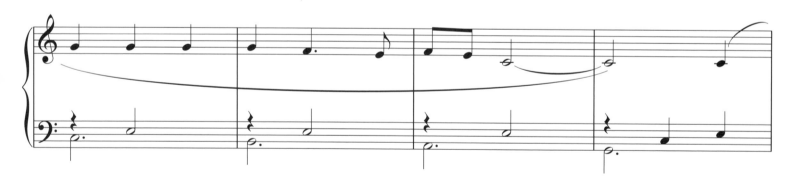

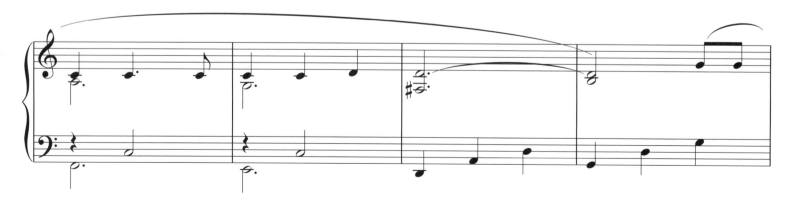

© 1973, 1974 (Renewed 2001, 2002) JOEL SONGS
This arrangement © 1987 JOEL SONGS
All Rights Reserved   International Copyright Secured   Used by Permission

YESTERDAY

Words and Music by JOHN LENNON
and PAUL McCARTNEY

Copyright © 1965 Sony/ATV Music Publishing LLC
Copyright Renewed
This arrangement Copyright © 1988 Sony/ATV Music Publishing LLC
All Rights Administered by Sony/ATV Music Publishing LLC, 8 Music Square West, Nashville, TN 37203
International Copyright Secured   All Rights Reserved

A FINE ROMANCE

from SWING TIME

Words by DOROTHY FIELDS
Music by JEROME KERN

Copyright © 1936 UNIVERSAL - POLYGRAM INTERNATIONAL PUBLISHING, INC. and ALDI MUSIC
Copyright Renewed
This arrangement Copyright © 1992 UNIVERSAL - POLYGRAM INTERNATIONAL PUBLISHING, INC. and ALDI MUSIC
Print Rights for ALDI MUSIC in the U.S. Controlled and Administered by HAPPY ASPEN MUSIC LLC c/o SHAPIRO, BERNSTEIN & CO., INC.
All Rights Reserved   Used by Permission

HOW DEEP IS THE OCEAN
(How High Is the Sky)

Words and Music by
IRVING BERLIN

© Copyright 1932 by Irving Berlin
Copyright Renewed
This arrangement © Copyright 2001 by the Estate of Irving Berlin
International Copyright Secured   All Rights Reserved

I'LL BE SEEING YOU

from RIGHT THIS WAY

Written by IRVING KAHAL
and SAMMY FAIN

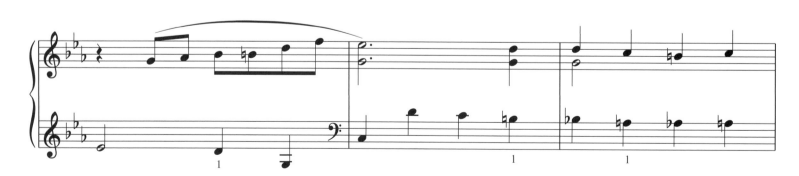

© 1938 (Renewed 1966, 1994) THE NEW IRVING KAHAL MUSIC (ASCAP)/Administered by BUG MUSIC and FAIN MUSIC CO.
This arrangement © 1995 THE NEW IRVING KAHAL MUSIC and FAIN MUSIC CO.
All Rights Reserved   Used by Permission

I'M ALWAYS CHASING RAINBOWS

Words by JOSEPH McCARTHY
Music by HARRY CARROLL

Copyright © 2010 by HAL LEONARD CORPORATION
International Copyright Secured   All Rights Reserved

SKYLARK

Words by JOHNNY MERCER
Music by HOAGY CARMICHAEL

Copyright © 1941, 1942 by Songs Of Peer, Ltd. and WB Music Corp.
Copyright Renewed
This arrangement Copyright © 2008 by Songs Of Peer, Ltd. and WB Music Corp.
International Copyright Secured   All Rights Reserved

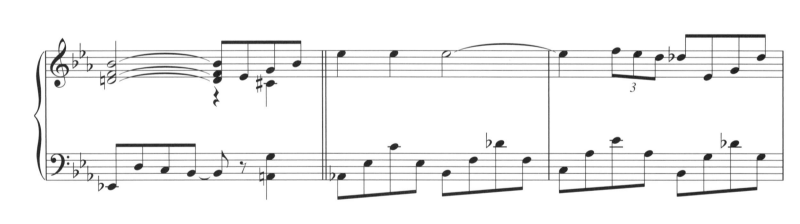

TENDERLY
from TORCH SONG

Lyric by JACK LAWRENCE
Music by WALTER GROSS

© 1946, 1947 EDWIN H. MORRIS & COMPANY, A Division of MPL Music Publishing, Inc.
Copyright Renewed, extended term of Copyright deriving from Jack Lawrence assigned and effective August 7, 2002 to RANGE ROAD MUSIC INC.
This arrangement © 2008 RANGE ROAD MUSIC INC.
All Rights Reserved

WHAT A WONDERFUL WORLD

Words and Music by GEORGE DAVID WEISS
and BOB THIELE

Slowly, with feeling

Copyright © 1967 by Range Road Music Inc., Bug Music-Quartet Music and Abilene Music, Inc.
Copyright Renewed
This arrangement Copyright © 2008 by Range Road Music Inc., Bug Music-Quartet Music and Abilene Music, Inc.
International Copyright Secured   All Rights Reserved
Used by Permission

257

AMAZING GRACE

Words by JOHN NEWTON
Traditional American Melody

Copyright © 1994 by HAL LEONARD CORPORATION
International Copyright Secured   All Rights Reserved

Flowing

a tempo

BATTLE HYMN OF THE REPUBLIC

Words by JULIA WARD HOWE
Music by WILLIAM STEFFE

March tempo, in 2

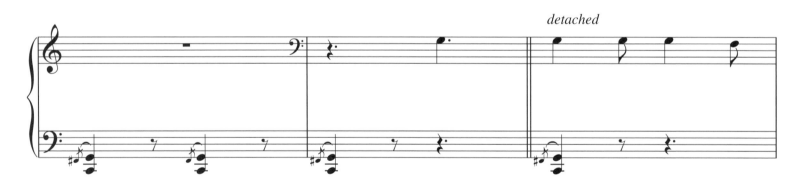

Copyright © 2010 by HAL LEONARD CORPORATION
International Copyright Secured   All Rights Reserved

WAYFARING STRANGER

Southern American Folk Hymn

Copyright © 2010 by HAL LEONARD CORPORATION
International Copyright Secured   All Rights Reserved

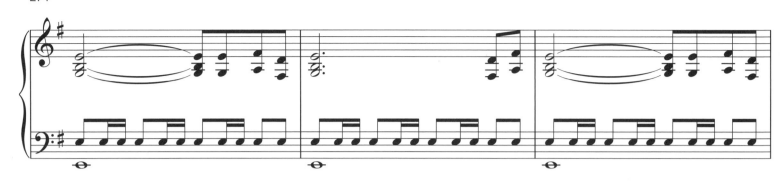

ZIP-A-DEE-DOO-DAH

from Walt Disney's SONG OF THE SOUTH

Words by RAY GILBERT
Music by ALLIE WRUBEL

Freely, in 2

Moderately fast

© 1945 Walt Disney Music Company
Copyright Renewed
This arrangement © 2010 Walt Disney Music Company
All Rights Reserved   Used by Permission

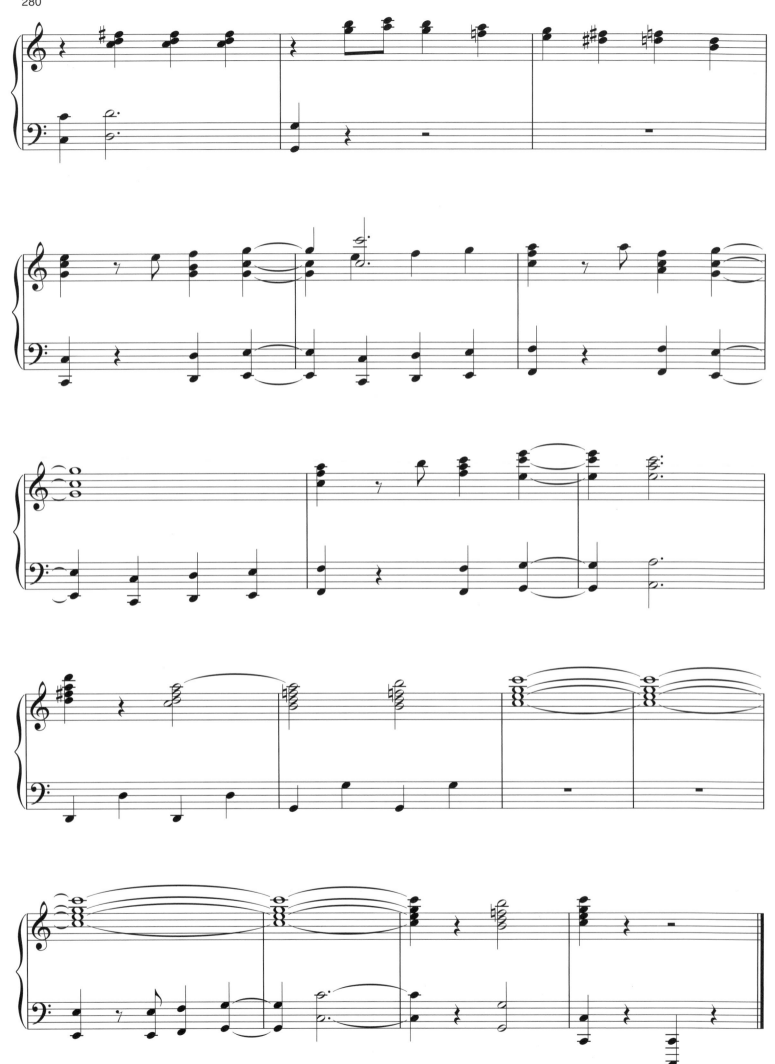